Fiddle Time Joggers

Piano accompaniment book

Kathy and David Blackwell

Teacher's note

These piano parts are written to accompany the tunes in *Fiddle Time Joggers*. They are an alternative to the violin duet accompaniments or audio tracks, and are not designed to be used with those items. With the exceptions of Nos. 4, 43, and 46, these parts may be used with violins playing together with violas (using *Viola Time Joggers* and playing the ensemble parts where appropriate); in a few pieces some details are different between the two books, for example some bar numbers and introductions. A separate viola piano accompaniment book is available providing parts for all the additional tunes in *Viola Time Joggers*.

Kathy and David Blackwell

OXFORD

UNIVERSITY PRESS

OXFORD
UNIVERSITY PRESS

Great Clarendon Street, Oxford OX2 6DP,
United Kingdom

Oxford University Press is a department of the University of Oxford.
It furthers the University's objective of excellence in research, scholarship,
and education by publishing worldwide. Oxford is a registered trade mark of
Oxford University Press in the UK and in certain other countries

ISBN 978-0-19-356213-4

Cover illustration by Martin Remphry

Music and text origination by Katie Johnston
Printed in Great Britain on acid-free paper by
Halstan & Co. Ltd, Amersham, Bucks.

Contents

1. Bow down, O Belinda

American folk tune

2. Under arrest!

KB & DB

3. Someone plucks, someone bows

Traditional
Words KB & DB

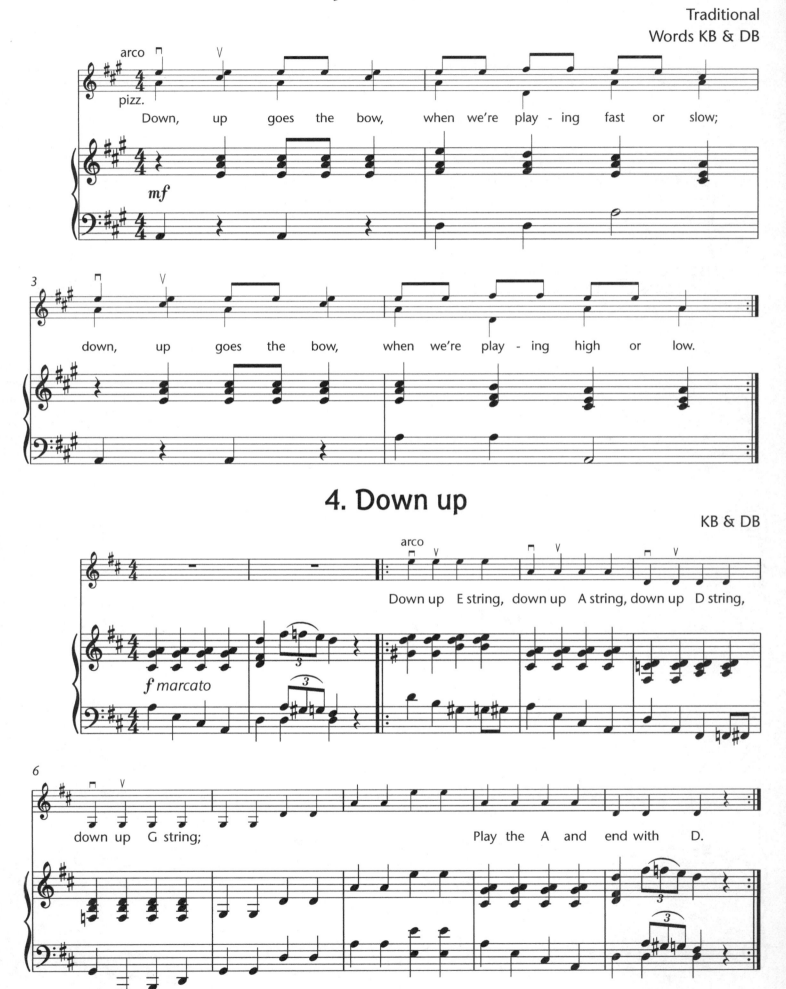

4. Down up

KB & DB

5. Two in a boat

American folk tune

6. London Bridge

English folk tune

2nd time: RH bars 1–4 8ve higher

I can play my o - pen D,

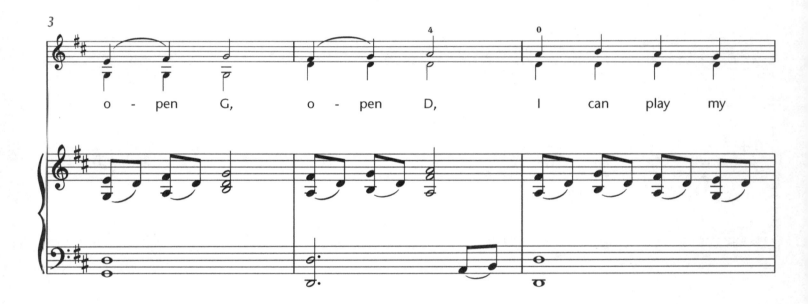

o - pen G, o - pen D, I can play my

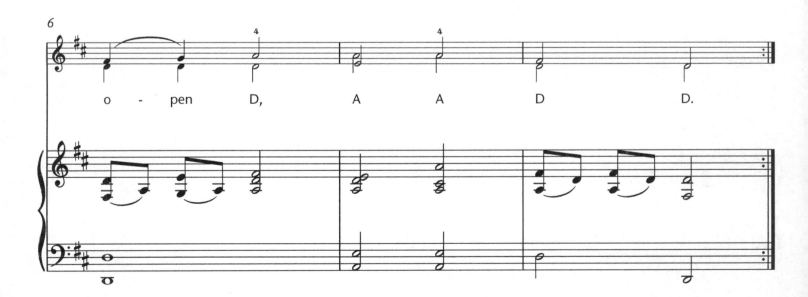

o - pen D, A A D D.

7. Fast lane

KB & DB

Try even faster the second time through!

8. In flight

KB & DB

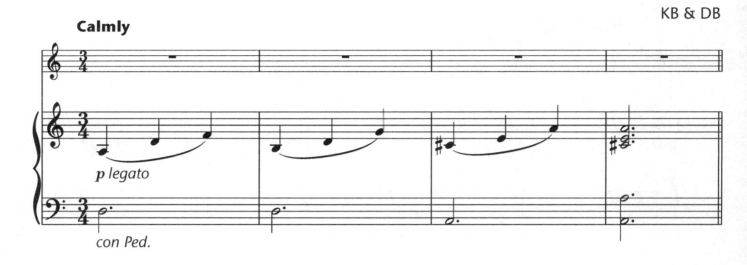

9. Lift off!

KB & DB

10. Katie's waltz

KB & DB

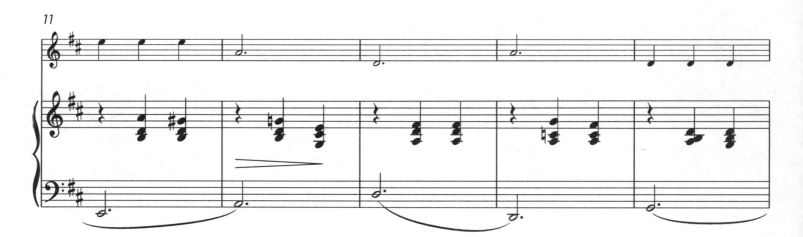

11. Copy cat

KB & DB

Can you play what I play? D D E E, D D E E,

Can you play what I play? Play it now with me.

Fine

Can you play what I play? A A B B, A A B B,

Can you play what I play? Play it now with me.

D.C. al Fine

12. Tap dancer

KB & DB

13. Rhythm fever

KB & DB

14. Here it comes!

KB & DB

15. So there!

KB & DB

So there!

16. Rowing boat

KB & DB

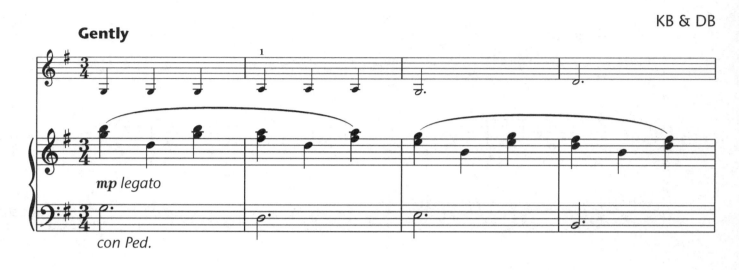

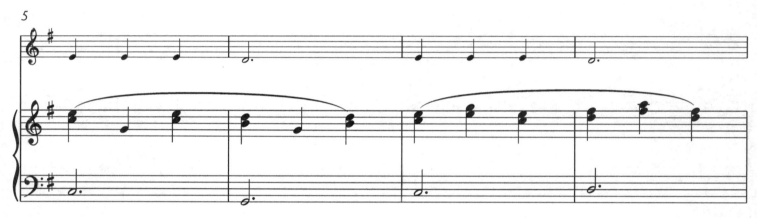

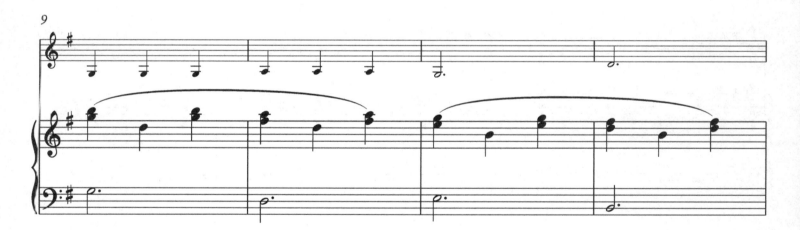

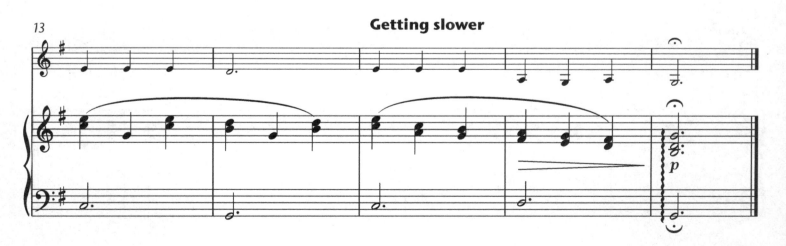

17. Ally bally

Scottish folk tune

18. Tiptoe, boo!

KB & DB

Tip - toe tip - toe   tip - toe, boo! (etc.)

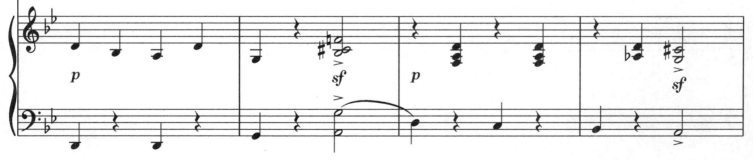

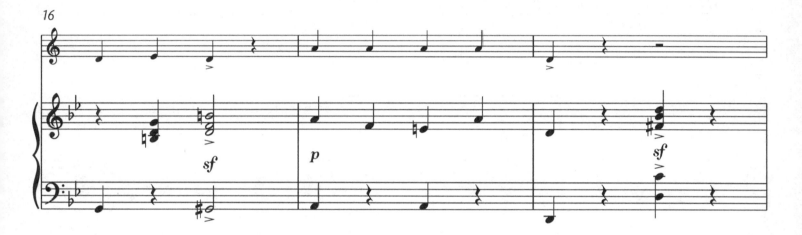

19. Travellin' slow

KB & DB

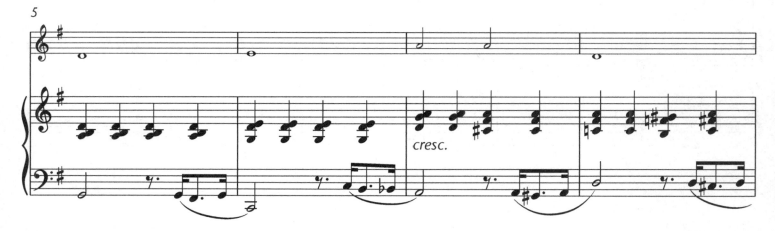

20. Lazy cowboy

KB & DB

21. Off to Paris

French folk tune

23. City lights

KB & DB

Nos. 22 and 23 are reversed to avoid a page turn.

22. Clare's song

KB & DB

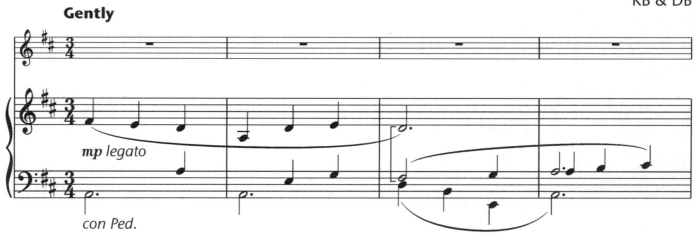

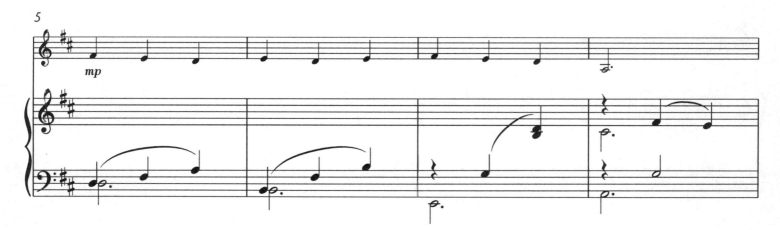

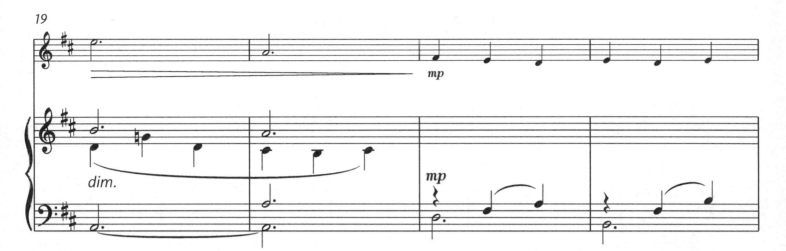

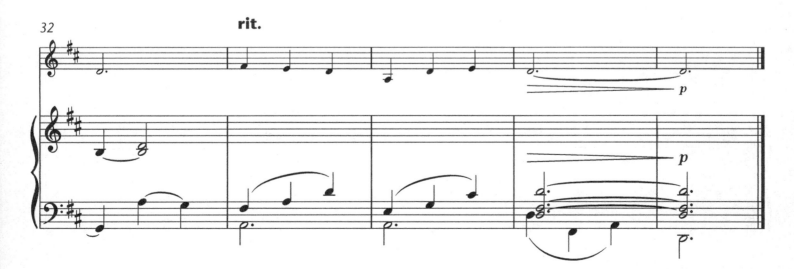

24. The three friends

Finnish folk tune

25. Peace garden

KB & DB

26. Summer sun

KB & DB

27. Phoebe in her petticoat

American folk tune

28. Ready, steady, go now!

KB & DB

29. Cooking in the kitchen

KB & DB

30. Happy go lucky (for Iain)

KB & DB

31. The mocking bird

American folk tune

Gently like a lullaby

rit.

32. Algy met a bear

KB & DB
Words anon.

Al - gy met a bear, a bear met Al - gy. The

bear was bul - gy, the bulge was Al - gy!

33. Listen to the rhythm

KB & DB

34. Cattle ranch blues

KB & DB

35. In the groove

KB & DB

36. Stamping dance

Czech folk tune

Heavily

37. Distant bells

KB & DB

38. Lazy scale

KB & DB

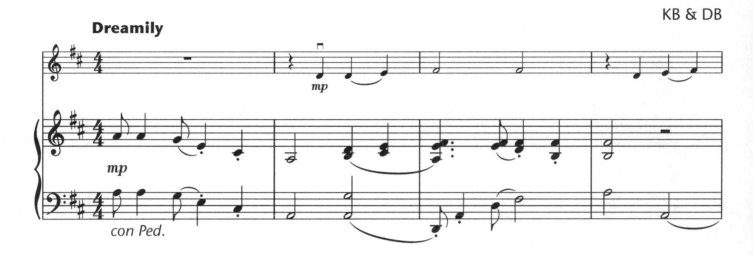

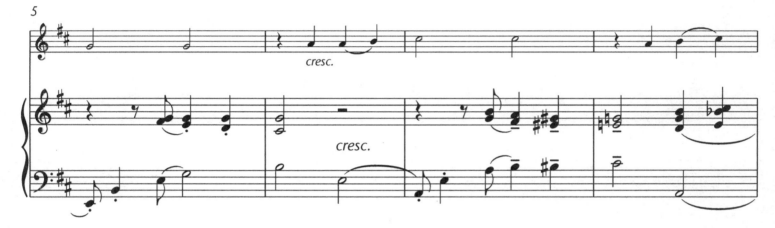

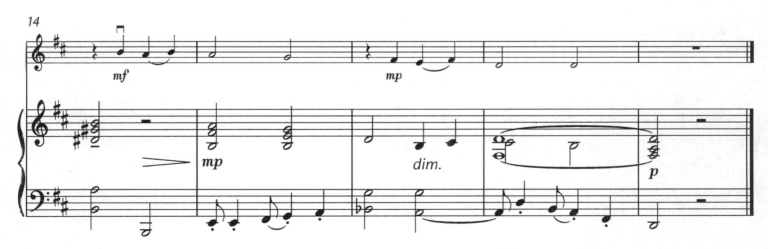

39. The old castle

KB & DB

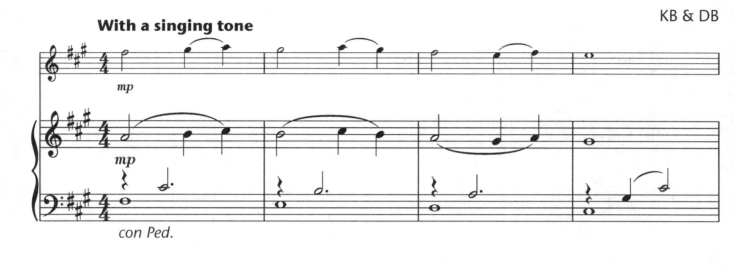

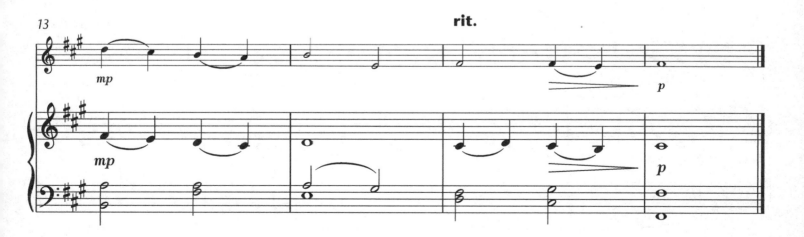

40. Rocking horse

KB & DB

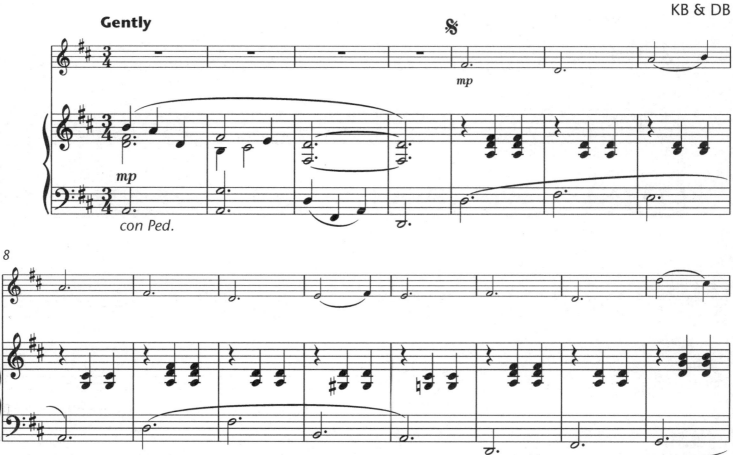

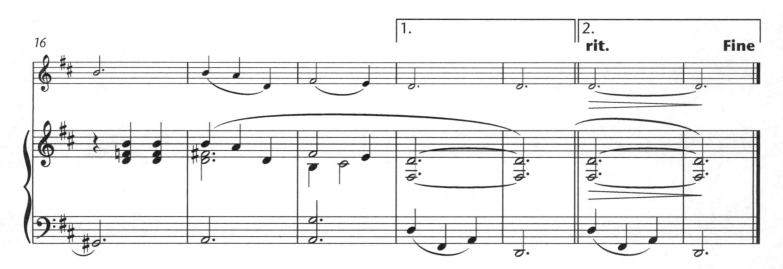

41. Patrick's reel

KB & DB

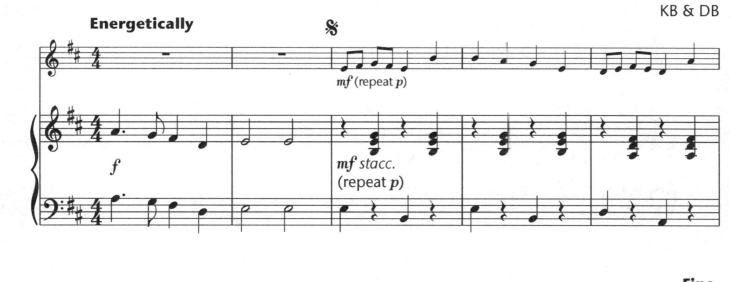

42. Calypso time

KB & DB

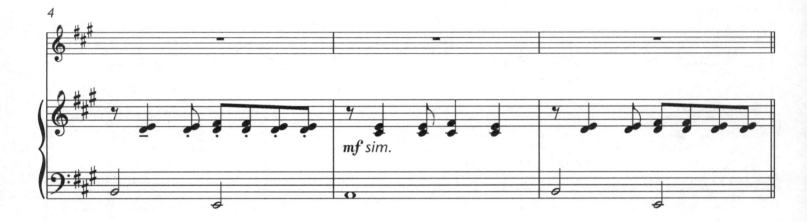

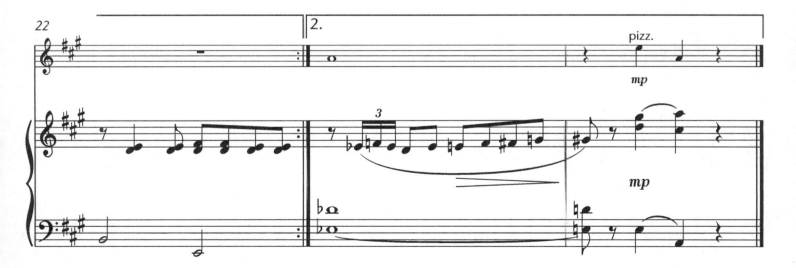

43. Knock, knock!

KB & DB

'Knock, knock.' 'Who's there?' 'Cook.' 'Cook who?' 'That's the first cuc-koo I've

heard this year!' 'Knock, knock.' 'Who's there?' 'Jes - ter.' 'Jes - ter who?'

'Jes-ter min-ute, I'll un - lock the door!'

44. Rocky mountain

American folk tune

45. Carrion crow

American folk tune

46. Flying high

KB & DB

47. Fiddle Time

KB & DB

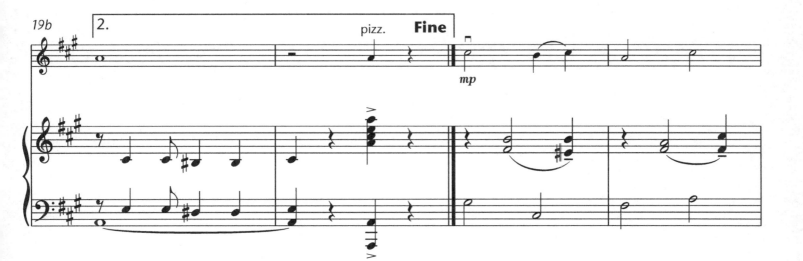